My Trip To Cuba

Travel Journal and Scrapbook

from
IronRingPublishing.com

Preserve your thoughts and memories forever!

Bring along *My Trip To Cuba* to journal your experiences while they're fresh in your head.

This travel journal and scrapbook contains some cheat sheets of the important tips and information contained in the bestselling *Travel To Cuba* guidebook (IronRingPublishing.com), and plenty of blank space for you to record your own daily diary so you can keep the memories of your dream vacation fresh for a lifetime!

Disclaimer and Terms of Use

IronRingPublishing.com

Emergency Contact Information –
Fill this out before you leave!

Contact #1:

Relationship:

Telephone:

Contact #2:

Relationship:

Telephone:

Contact #3:

Relationship:

Telephone:

Doctor's name:

Doctor's telephone:

Interesting Facts About Cuba

1. Cubans nicknamed their country the 'Crocodile Island', because when you look at it from the air, it really does appear like a crocodile.

2. The infamous military prison, Guantanamo Bay, is in Cuba, although on US soil. Actually, the United States is renting this area from Cuba for a bit over $4,000 per month. Cuba hasn't cashed any of the checks yet.

3. The official name of CIA plan for deposing Fidel Castro was 'Castration'.

4. There are lots of American cars from the 50's on the streets of Havana. However, in most cases, only the shell is US-made, with the engine being taken from Soviet cars from the 70's.

5. Government cars are obligated by law to pick up hitchhikers.

6. Cuba is the land of cigars, and at least one in three Cubans is a smoker. Nearly one fifth of Cubans between thirteen and fifteen years of age are smokers.

7. Cuban seniors have a special deal with the state about buying cigars – every month they can get three cigars for approximately a dime.

8. Buying souvenirs from a local vendor will not put money directly into their pocket. Cuba is a socialist state, so everything is common property, including souvenirs.

9. Only one in twenty Cubans has access to Internet and up until 2008, cell phones were banned on the island.

10. Education and health care in Cuba are among the best in the world. Cuba is among the countries with the highest literacy rates with 99.8%.

11. The popular myth that Christmas is banned in Cuba is false. Christmas became an official holiday in 1997.

12. Despite being a secular state and promoting atheism, the majority of Cubans are practicing Catholics. In the last couple of years, there has been an increase in the number of Cuban people practicing Santeria, an Afro-Caribbean religion.

13. Europeans first tried chocolate in Cuba. It was reserved for rich Spaniards and aristocracy for almost the whole 16th century.

Places you should consider visiting in Cuba:

- ☐ Old Havana ("La Habana Vieja")

- ☐ Castillo de la Real Fuerza

- ☐ Malecon

- ☐ Museum of the Revolution

- ☐ Che Guevara Mausoleum

- ☐ Trinidad

- ☐ Zapata Swamp

- ☐ Pico Turquino

- ☐ Romeo y Julieta cigar factory tour

Recommended Restaurants in Havana and Old Habana:

- ☐ Floridita
- ☐ La Bodeguita del Medio
- ☐ Nazdarovie
- ☐ San Cristobal
- ☐ Coppelia

Survival Spanish Phrases

Not many locals in Cuba speak English, so it's best to learn a few useful phrases:

Estoy perdido (es'toi peɾ'ðiðo) - I am lost (if you're male)
Estoy perdida (es'toi peɾ'ðiða) - I am lost (if you're female)

¿Dónde está el aeropuerto? ('donde es'ta el aeɾo'pweɾto) - Where is the airport?

¿Cuándo sale el vuelo? ('kwando 'sale el 'βwelo) - When does the flight leave?

¿Cuándo llega el vuelo? ('kwando 'ʎeɣa el 'βwelo) - When does the flight arrive?

¿Dónde está mi hotel? ('donde es'ta mi o'tel) - Where is my hotel?

Mis maletas están perdidas (miz ma'letas es'tam peɾ'ðiðas) - My suitcases are lost

Yo necesito un taxi (ɟo neθe'sito un ta'khsi) - I need a taxi

¿Dónde está la estación de ferrocarril? ('donde es'ta la esta'θjon de feroka'ril) - Where is the bus/train station?

¿Cuánto es el pasaje? ('kwanto es el pa'saxe) - How much is the fare?

Necesito agua (neθe'sito 'aɣwa) - I need water

Tengo hambre ('teŋgo 'ambɾe) - I'm hungry

¿Dónde están los baños públicos? ('donde es'tan loz 'baɲos 'puβlikos) - Where are the public bathrooms?

Know Before You Go – Practical Tips for Travel to Cuba

Visas and Passports

Before a trip to Cuba, visitors must obtain a tourist card in one of the Cuban diplomatic missions. Almost any tourist agency can do this for you. Citizens of Canada get the Cuban tourist card on board the airplane, as it is included in the price of the airfare. With a tourist card, you can stay 30 days in Cuba (Canadians can stay three times longer), with a possibility of doubling up that period. There are nineteen countries whose citizens are exempt for getting a visa for traveling to Cuba. The list includes Russia, China, and a number of Asian and African countries. Apart from the tourist card, it is necessary to have a valid passport with you. It is recommended to have at least six months remaining before renewing the passport, in order to avoid any complications.

US citizens who want to visit Cuba must have a passport with them that is valid at least 180 days after the trip. Another condition is having the tourist card, which costs about $25. US citizens are also required to have a proof that they've purchased a return ticket. Those three conditions are imposed by Cuba, but Americans have to get a permit from their own country as well. The U.S. Treasury Department requires the travelers to obtain special permission. Since January 2015, the requirements are much more relaxed and the tourist permit is not hard to get.

Credit Cards and Cash

There are two official currencies in Cuba, the Cuban peso (MN) and the convertible peso (CUC). MN or 'Moneda Nacional' as its official name is, is used by the locals, while CUC is reserved for tourists. The prices in MN are controlled by the government, so they are far lower than prices reserved for tourists. For example, a Cuban can get six cans of beer for an equivalent of one US dollar. Because of that, it would be ideal if you managed to exchange your national currency for MN, but that option doesn't exist in official exchange offices, where you can only purchase the convertible peso (CUC). Instead, you would need to find a local who is ready to accept your currency. So, be friendly to everyone and you could spend your Cuban days in luxury!

The CUC currency is commonly referred to as a "dollar" as the conversion between CUC and the US dollar is 1:1.

Because of the US embargo on Cuba, no credit or debit cards issued by banks with any connection to the United States can be used on the island. MasterCard has announced in the early 2015 that they are planning to lift the restrictions in the near future. Visa cards issued by non-US banks can be used all over Cuba.

A large majority of hotels allows paying with cards, but this isn't the case in most of the shops, bars, and restaurants in Cuba. Cards can be used to withdraw cash from ATMs, but be aware that there aren't many of them in Cuba. You will be sure to find them at the airport, hotels and resorts, and in proximity of main tourist sites, but elsewhere it's better to have cash in your pockets.

International Phone

Public phones are all around big Cuban cities like Havana, Santiago de Cuba, and Santa Clara. You can also find a lot of them in tourist resort towns like Varadero and Jardines del Rey. Public telephones are a fairly cheap way to phone home. To call abroad from Cuba, travelers need to buy a telephone card, which costs 20 CUC. For that money, you will basically solve the phone issue for the whole length of your stay. Using your cell phone to call home is not a good idea as it might be very expensive. To stay in contact with your fellow companions in Cuba, it might be wise getting a prepaid Cuban SIM card. The rates are very attractive: 0.30 CUC per minute for a call between two cell phones located in Cuba; calling abroad will probably cost you between $1.60 and $1.80 per minute.

Internet

The lack of internet access to the majority of Cubans is a proof that Cuba is still a totalitarian state. Only about five percent of Cubans use the internet, and the limited service that is available is very closely monitored. Being a foreigner, you are allowed to go online, but the problem is there aren't many places where you can do that. The airport, 5-star hotels, and some luxury restaurants, especially those in the capital city, might have internet access. But keep in mind that the internet is extremely slow here, a sort of speed it had in the 1990's in other parts of the world. Also some programs you're used to, like Skype, for example, are not available in Cuba. Another downside is that it is pretty expensive. Hotels, for example offer WI-FI for rates of 8 CUC per hour.

In the last few years, the Cuban government started setting up so-called telepuntos. These are basically state-owned public premises that have computers with internet access. Telepuntos work on the same principle as public phones. You are required to buy an internet card and use it to turn on a telepunto. The rate is 6 CUC per one hour, which is less pricey than WI-FI. The bad thing about telepuntos is that you cannot use your personal computer or smart phone, but only their computers.

Travel Insurance

Travelers visiting Cuba are advised to have travel insurance, not only because of their protection in case the unexpected happens, but also to avoid any problems with obtaining Cuban tourist card. Actually, for citizens of some countries, a travel medical insurance is required. People from the United States will not even get permission to travel to Cuba from the US Treasury Department if they don't have valid insurance. Without it, they are not allowed to enter Cuba, so it is wise to solve that while you're still in your home country. An alternative is to get the insurance from a local Cuban company.

Getting Around: Renting a Car in Cuba, Public Transportation

You will be stunned by the cars you'll see on the Cuban. There isn't a city on the planet with as many American old-timers as Havana. The story behind this is that Cuban capital was crowded with US-made cars during the 1950's. But, since the US embargo started, the import of American cars to Cuba stopped. Because of that, Cubans had to take care of what they got. The other alternative was getting a car from the Soviet Union or Eastern Germany, like Lada or Wartburg. Today, you can see both the old American cars and Russian cars from the 70's and 80's on Cuban streets. You can ride in them if you grab a taxi, which are all government owned. Taxi fares are rarely higher than 0.50 CUC per kilometer. You can travel between cities by bus or a car on one of eight expressways in the country, six of which are connected with the capital.

Taxis are mainly used by tourists, while the locals use public buses. Cuban public transportation is an interesting and colorful system with vehicles brought from all over the world. In Havana, you can see American yellow school buses that were imported from Canada, trailer buses from China, and buses previously used in the Netherlands, Spain, and Belarus. In addition, there are many privately-owned 'buses', which might not be proper to call them that. These vehicles are improvised buses made of cars or trucks.

For long-distance traveling on the island, Cubans often use trains. Although the majority of train routes use outdated locomotives, there are some that are of a higher standard. The passenger train Havana-Santiago is one of those.

Customs Regulations (What You Can Bring, What You Can Take Out)

Obviously, you can't bring dangerous things like narcotics, weapons, or explosives into Cuba. But apart from the things that are banned all over the world, Cuba has a few more forbidden items. You are not allowed to import any kind of pornographic material, nor books and documents directed against Cuba and its communist system. Also, you cannot bring in a number of household appliances, including cooking plates, microwave ovens, toasters, or electric irons. Things you are allowed to bring in, besides your personal belongings, include 200 cigarettes (or 50 cigars) and 3 bottles of alcoholic beverage.

Without paying export fees, you can take out of Cuba 200 cigarettes (or 50 cigars), 5 bottles of alcoholic beverage, and souvenirs of the value up to $1,000 USD. The citizens of the United States who are leaving Cuba are allowed to take out cigars up to $100 dollars value. Among things that are strictly prohibited for export is Cuban money.

Weather and What to Wear

Cuba is a tropical island, and such has a dry and a wet season over the course of a year. You probably want to visit this country when the weather conditions are favorable, so you should look to book your trip somewhere between December and May. During these six months, the average low temperature ranges from 65 to 72 °F, while the average high goes from 78 to 86 °F. In the other half of the year, temperatures are a bit lower (except August which is the hottest month with the average high of 89 °F) and rain is happening often. The average rainfall is highest in June and October, while hurricanes are also a common sight during the wet season. Throughout the year, temperature rarely goes below 50 °F, so in most cases, you should pack summer clothes.

Date: _____

Location: _____

Notes, memories, and experiences:

Notes, memories, and experiences:

Paste photos below:

Paste photos below:

Date: _____

Location: _____

Notes, memories, and experiences:

Notes, memories, and experiences:

Paste photos below:

Paste photos below:

Date: _____

Location: _____

Notes, memories, and experiences:

Notes, memories, and experiences:

IronRingPublishing.com

Paste photos below:

Paste photos below:

Date: _____

Location: _____

Notes, memories, and experiences:

Notes, memories, and experiences:

Paste photos below:

Paste photos below:

Date: _____

Location: _____

Notes, memories, and experiences:

Notes, memories, and experiences:

Paste photos below:

Paste photos below:

Date: _____

Location: _____

Notes, memories, and experiences:

Notes, memories, and experiences:

Paste photos below:

Paste photos below:

Date: _____

Location: _____

Notes, memories, and experiences:

Notes, memories, and experiences:

Paste photos below:

IronRingPublishing.com

Paste photos below:

Date: _____

Location: _____

Notes, memories, and experiences:

Notes, memories, and experiences:

Paste photos below:

Paste photos below:

Date: _____

Location: _____

Notes, memories, and experiences:

Notes, memories, and experiences:

Paste photos below:

Paste photos below:

Date: _____

Location: _____

Notes, memories, and experiences:

Notes, memories, and experiences:

Paste photos below:

Paste photos below:

Date: _____

Location: _____

Notes, memories, and experiences:

Notes, memories, and experiences:

Paste photos below:

Paste photos below:

Date: _____

Location: _____

Notes, memories, and experiences:

Notes, memories, and experiences:

Paste photos below:

Paste photos below:

Date: _____

Location: _____

Notes, memories, and experiences:

Notes, memories, and experiences:

Paste photos below:

Paste photos below:

Date: _____

Location: _____

Notes, memories, and experiences:

Notes, memories, and experiences:

Paste photos below:

Paste photos below:

Date: _____

Location: _____

Notes, memories, and experiences:

Notes, memories, and experiences:

Paste photos below:

Paste photos below:

Date: _____

Location: _____

Notes, memories, and experiences:

Notes, memories, and experiences:

Paste photos below:

Paste photos below:

Date: _____

Location: _____

Notes, memories, and experiences:

Notes, memories, and experiences:

Paste photos below:

Paste photos below:

Date: _____

Location: _____

Notes, memories, and experiences:

Notes, memories, and experiences:

Paste photos below:

Paste photos below:

Date: _____

Location: _____

Notes, memories, and experiences:

Notes, memories, and experiences:

Paste photos below:

Paste photos below:

Date: _____

Location: _____

Notes, memories, and experiences:

Notes, memories, and experiences:

Paste photos below:

Paste photos below:

Date: _____

Location: _____

Notes, memories, and experiences:

Notes, memories, and experiences:

Paste photos below:

Paste photos below:

Date: _____

Location: _____

Notes, memories, and experiences:

Notes, memories, and experiences:

Paste photos below:

Paste photos below:

Date: _____

Location: _____

Notes, memories, and experiences:

Notes, memories, and experiences:

Paste photos below:

Paste photos below:

Made in the USA
San Bernardino, CA
08 April 2018